This book was written for my dear friend,
Jennifer Janine Stephens
who showed us the true meaning of strength and faith
in her struggle against melanoma cancer.

This book is dedicated to all those who
battle illness with bravery, determination and hope.

Kathy

Library of Congress Cataloging-in Publication Data

Cramer, Kathy, 1961-
     If I could be sick for you for Just One Day / written by
Kathy Cramer ; illustrated by Steve Harmon
          p. cm.
     ISBN 0-9726504-7-4 (alk. paper)
          1. Consolation – Poetry 2. Sick – Poetry
          I. Title: Just One Day. II. Harmon, Steve, 1961- III. Title.
     PS3603.R364I37 2005
     811'.6—dc22   2005045953

TRISTAN Publishing
2355 Louisiana Avenue North
Golden Valley, MN 55427

ISBN 0-9726504-7-4
Printed in China
Second Printing

For Marge.
Who gave so much.
- Jennifer, Steve,
Cole and Ava

Kelly you are the reason this book has
become a reality. Thank you for your
loving support, your amazing talent and
your compassion for others. Love you
more than publishing our first book.
                                        - Mom

If I could be sick for you

for

Just One Day

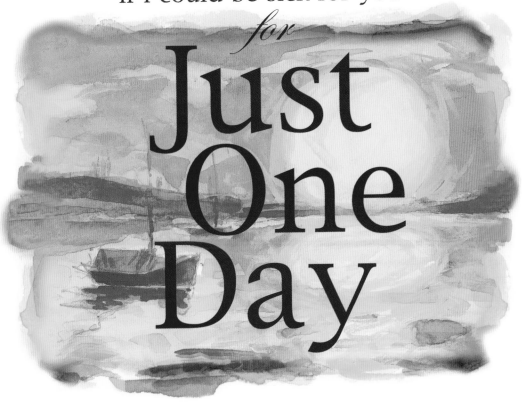

Written by Kathy Cramer
Illustrated by Steve Harmon

TRISTAN Publishing
Minneapolis

I wish I could be sick for you
for just one day.

I would let you go outside and run and play!

I would swallow the pills
   that don't want to stay down.

You could stick your head out the window
and ride all over town.

I would shake and chill the way you do.

You could go sail on a sailboat -
be part of the crew!

I would feel the pain
that you endure.

You could go out for a big dinner...
order dessert, for sure.

I would dream the dreams that
can be scary and dark.

You could fish on a lake
and walk through the park.

I would do your wishing to feel better soon.

You could stay up late
and sleep until noon.

I would look through the cards
that were sent by friends.

You could eat popcorn and
candy until a movie begins.

I would walk your path
with heavy tired steps.

You could drink lemonade
and sit out on the deck.

I would feel the faith that
you hold in your heart.

You could walk
through the market,
smell the flowers
on a cart.

I would eat the food that
doesn't taste right.

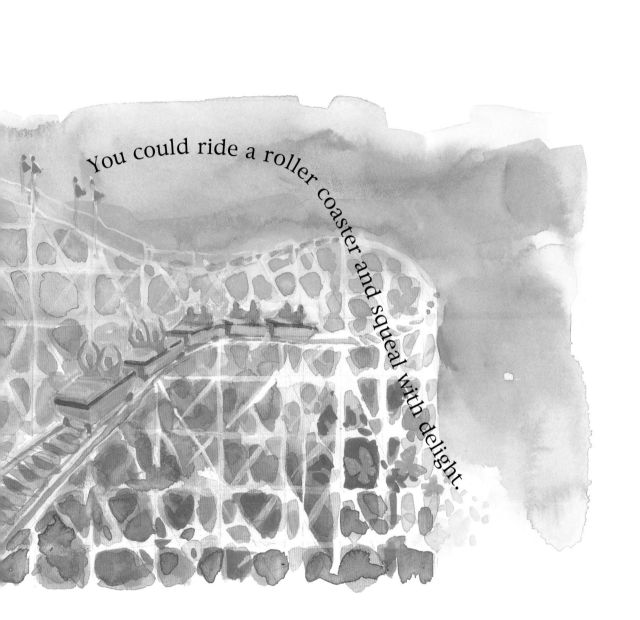

You could ride a roller coaster and squeal with delight.

I would look out your window
and wonder why.

You could visit all your friends
just to say "Hi!"

I would hold your anger
that comes and goes.

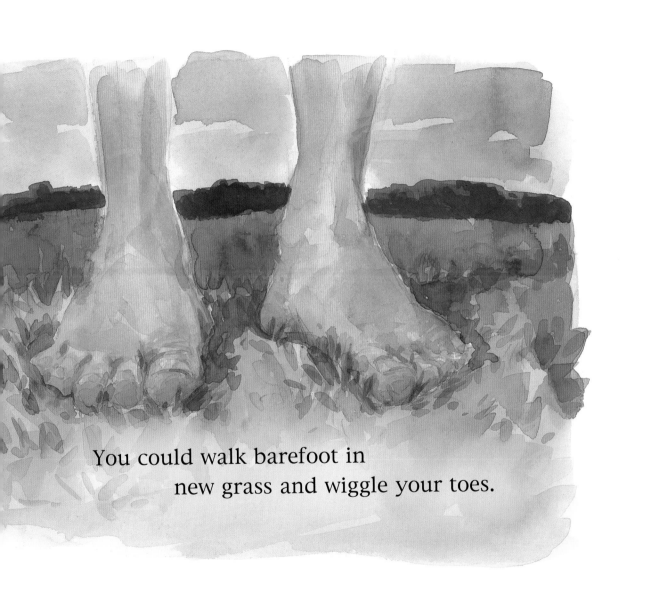

You could walk barefoot in
    new grass and wiggle your toes.

I would do your
wondering of
what is to be.

You could read a book
under a big shady tree.

I would listen to the footsteps
that come and go.

You could sit by the fire
        or play in the snow.

I would lie in your bed
    for that day and night.

        You could sit and watch
            a sunset, blazing
                and bright.

I wish I could be sick for you
for just one day.

But since I can't...
by your side I will stay.